RELEASING RELIGION

I0617291

How to Become a Better Christian

Jessica T. Grier

Getting On Higher Ground Media
8170 Mall Pkwy, # 1251
Lithonia, GA 30038
highergroundconsulting.co
info@highergroundconsulting.co

COPYRIGHT

Library of Congress Control Number: 2023913182
Printed in the United States of America.
ISBN- 979-8-9876240-1-2

Getting on Higher Ground Media
Lithonia, GA

DEDICATIONS

I give all praise, honor, and glory to God the Father,
Son, and Holy Spirit for this inspirational work.
May it be a blessing to the Kingdom.

To all the people who have ever thought
outside of the box, who didn't accept the status quo,
and put forth a good faith effort to try to understand
the purpose of life and how to live it well
and please God.

To the members of my incredibly supportive
launch team, thank you! I know this book will
reach even more people because of your help:
Ashley H., Asia E., Kandace L., Shavien S.,
and Pastor Keisha. I also want to thank
my mom, Julia, and husband, Darrius
for your constant love and support!

PRAYER

I pray that you allow yourself to be open to the perspective I share in this book. Know that in my heart, I want you to truly know the God you serve and to serve Him with all of your heart. May this be the beginning of the journey of a lifetime.

CONTENTS
Table of

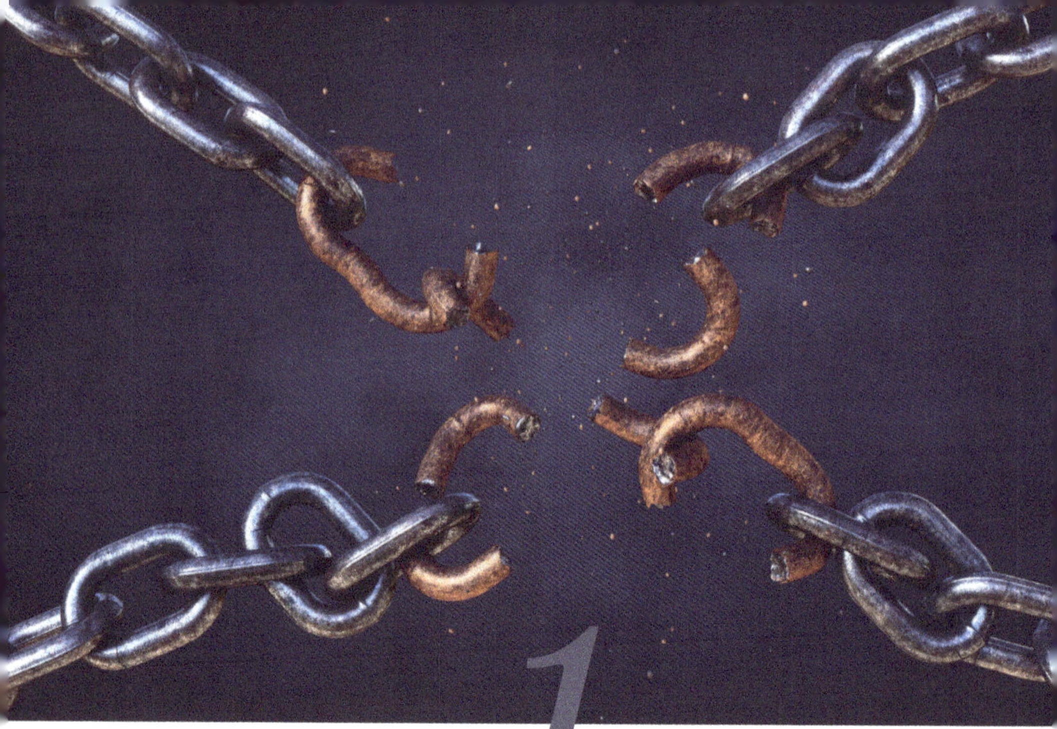

1

INTRODUCTION

I've been a church-attending Christian for as long as I can remember. I did everything I was expected to do as a Christian. I had always gone to church, been heavily involved in ministries, served as a long-time member, listened to sermons, learned scripture occasionally, treated people fairly, tithed, and I thought I was doing good. Until one day I realized that I wasn't as good of a Christian as I thought I was. I really didn't know the Bible for myself and therefore let church culture influence me more than the Word of God.

 Did my peers even know I believed in Jesus?!

I rarely prayed outside of blessing my food, I never witnessed, and most importantly I did not have an intimate relationship with God.

The truth in that moment is that I was just passing for a Christian on the outside, but I really did not know Jesus in my heart. My faith sucked. I had a works mentality and had gained little true value being a church member all this time. This was a hard pill to swallow, and it was at that moment sitting in another routine church service that I made the decision to do better, to be a better Christian and to really take this walk seriously because God deserved better.

Years later, as I reflect on my journey, I realize how common my experience was and still is. As much as I have grown and developed in my relationship with God, I want other Christians to experience the same. I want others to realize how much God wants to be involved in their lives. This is not about theology, denominations, or the universal church.

This is not an opportunity for self-shame. This is an invitation to becoming better in practical ways. We will not be creating a lofty list of goals that you need to complete in 30 days. This is not that kind of book. We will address some misconceptions, measure our lives up to the standards of the Bible, and take actionable steps to grow personally.

This is about you and God, what you need from Him, and what He wants from you. This is about how you become better through your active faith in Jesus Christ.

2

MINDSET MYTHS

Before we get to the practical steps you need to take to become a better Christian, we need to review some myths that, if not addressed, will prevent you from growing.

<u>Myth #1</u>: It takes too much time!

Most people believe that they don't have the time to commit to the lifestyle they proclaim to desire. Have you ever wondered what that sounds like to God? You say, "I want to be closer to God and hear from him, I just don't have the time like other people do."

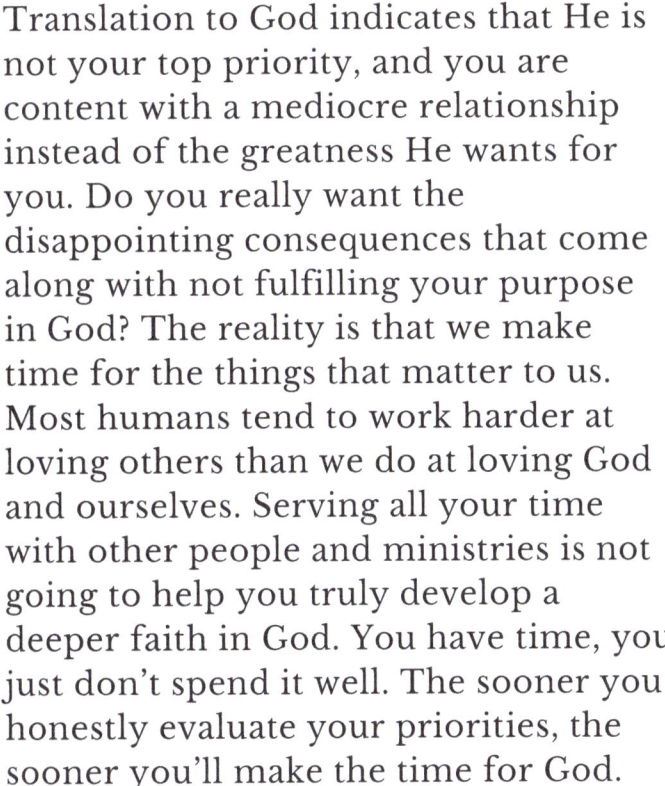

Translation to God indicates that He is not your top priority, and you are content with a mediocre relationship instead of the greatness He wants for you. Do you really want the disappointing consequences that come along with not fulfilling your purpose in God? The reality is that we make time for the things that matter to us. Most humans tend to work harder at loving others than we do at loving God and ourselves. Serving all your time with other people and ministries is not going to help you truly develop a deeper faith in God. You have time, you just don't spend it well. The sooner you honestly evaluate your priorities, the sooner you'll make the time for God.

Myth #2: If only I had the anointing like "(insert name of a highly revered person)" and I'll be good to go.

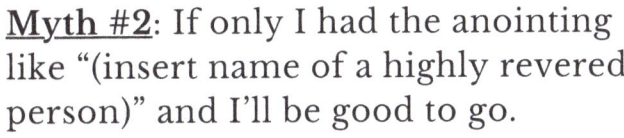

God gave you the same gift of salvation through Christ and the gift of the Holy Spirit to do everything you need. It's already in you, you simply need to activate your faith and go forth. We tend to look at others and admire the life of perfection they live from our perspective. Reality is that no one is better than another person.

You are enough for God to use as He wills. Yes, with all your baggage, insecurities, trauma, pride, etc. God is still willing to use YOU. Of course, there is always more you can learn, but God is not looking for perfection or qualifications; He's looking for a willing heart.

It's time to stop this cycle of fake humility you're experiencing and really trust God to use even you to do impossible things. He will use the little that you have to do far more than you ever imagined. You don't need more anointing; you just need to take the time to hear from God and obey.

Myth #3: Failure is wrong

Sometimes we confuse failure for sin. Making a mistake and failing at your attempt at life is not necessarily a sin. I think that sometimes people are so scared of being great that they hold on to minor flaws as proof that they can't be used.

Failure serves the purpose of reminding us that we are in need of the One who knows all and is all. You are not a bad person because you made a mistake, you reacted too quickly, or failed at something.

Failure simply means that you are human, and you need God's love to thrive, not validation from people. God's love is patient and kind. There is a difference between how you have been programmed to respond to failure through guilt and shame and how God loves you through every circumstance.

Love is patient, love is kind. It does not envy, it does not boast, it is not proud. It does not dishonor others, it is not self-seeking, it is not easily angered, it keeps no record of wrongs. Love does not delight in evil but rejoices with the truth. It always protects, always trusts, always hopes, always perseveres.

1 Corinthians 13: 4-7, NIV

Use your failures as a reminder to stay on track with God and to wait for His timing.

Mindset Myths vs. Truths

Now that I have identified a few common myths among Believers, it is time for you to identify the lies you encounter in your private thoughts. Write additional myths on the left side and truths on the right side. I have given a few examples to get you started.

Myth of the Enemy	Truth of God
I don't have time for myself.	I am a great manager of my time. Colossians 4:5
God doesn't care about my small problems.	God is El Roi- The God who sees me. Genesis 13:16
I am a mistake.	I was formed and set apart by God. Jeremiah 1:5

Use the truths you have written as personal affirmations!

Chart Your Course to Success with a Free Kingdom Wellness Planning Session

Kingdom Wellness Coaching is a wholistic approach to spiritual direction and wellness designed to help Believers apply God's Word to every area of their life within nine unique areas. I, Jessica T. Grier, am offering you an amazing opportunity to jumpstart your journey with a Free Kingdom Wellness Planning Session!

This complimentary call is designed to help you identify your top three areas of focus and actionable steps you can take immediately. You deserve to walk in the authority God has given you and we can help you get your life in order and regain control.

Schedule a call by scanning the QR code or visit calendly.com/gettingon higherground

But that's not all! After our discussion, I'll also provide some background about myself, my expertise, and my approach to coaching. If by the end of our conversation, I am confident that I can be of assistance, I will share details on how we can continue working together. Should you choose to proceed, that's amazing. If not, there's absolutely no pressure. Regardless of your decision, you'll walk away from our session with a well-defined plan of action to follow, empowering you to take the next steps in your journey.

3

PERSONAL PERSPECTIVES

So let me preface the remaining material with a few explanations about my personal perspectives to eliminate any confusion.

1) I believe in the God of the Holy Bible, and He has taught me so that I can share my light with others. I love God the Father- Yah. I follow Him. I am saved by the blood of His Son-

Jesus Christ of Nazareth- Yeshua, who died on the cross and was resur- rected. I believe that a gift from God is His Holy Spirit which dwells in me as a Believer.

2) My goal is to share my experience so that others can walk in boldness. This will naturally cause division because there is a clear right and wrong.

My job is not to condemn others for their past positions or decisions, but rather to shed light on the truth so people can make the proper decisions for themselves.

3) The church in this book refers to the mainstream church religion that most Christians are influenced by. The kind you see in movies and television. The kind that have typical Sunday services, decently large congregations, offer various ministries, and participate in praise and worship, giving, and sermons regularly. They host regular services and activities for kids and youth, hire ministers to handle different needs of the congregation, and from the outside seem to run smoothly. The normal American church.

It doesn't matter what city you're in, your demographics, the size of your steeple, or your denomination; almost everyone is familiar with the typical "church".

There are a good number of people who understand that the church mentioned in #3 is a religion. The people who attend a physical church may refer to themselves as Christians, but most of them are more influenced by and committed to the church as a religion than they are influenced by Christ as their center. I want people to release the bondage of this church religion and embrace what it truly means to be a Believer in Jesus Christ, the Messiah.

By religion, I'm referring to the dictionary.com definition of a specific fundamental set of beliefs and practices generally agreed upon by a number of persons or sects

The mainstream church has become a religion. It has its own set of beliefs and practices separate from the Christian faith detailed in the Bible. Most of its rules are unwritten but well understood through tradition. It is a social organization used for entertaining attendees and ceremonial purposes of the people within that community rather than a holy house of prayer. This is not a shot at anyone in particular; it's just an observation of the toxic system that has developed to deceive Christians of their true faith.

Before you continue reading, I just want to remind you that I'm speaking from my experience as well, as I was once in the same position- more familiar with church than Christ. I chose to change, and you can too.

4

THE CHRISTIANESE CAMP

Most church attendees speak Christianese, meaning that they pass as a Christian to the general public because they know all the verbiage to appear to be a true believer. They carry a Bible, dress nicely, stand at the right times, clap to the music, encourage the preacher to "talk good", say "Amen" at the end of prayer, and throw in a "Hallelujah" at just the right moment to indicate they are in tune with what's going on. They volunteer to help others, serve on the usher board or hospitality committee, organize special events, and genuinely enjoy the community they are in; no matter how shallow it is. Some even know how to shout, pray eloquently, and speak in tongues.

On the flip side, they are also living in sin and only work to hide it from those they consider "brothers and sisters in Christ". They would never confess sin out of fear of judgment and being ostracized, thus enslaving themselves to tradition and further bondage.

They are completely different people at church, school, work, and home, which really makes it difficult for them to identify who they truly are.

The sermons they hear on Sundays are usually considered good because they pertain to other people's problems and not theirs. They come to church to wear a mask and present themselves as perfect. They believe that God is real but have little faith that He will work in their lives, so much so that they take notes on the sermon on Sunday but are back to believing science has the only answers on Monday. Their church community means a lot to them, more than their independent relationship with God. They are proud members of their church, but it's a stretch to say they are true Ambassadors for Christ.

They live the definition of insanity-doing the same thing over and over again every year, expecting a different result. Every year another dream dies, and hope is deferred, but they keep trying the same things because it's what everyone else is doing (The Wide Gate). I wonder if people have ever considered another route- the road less traveled (The Narrow Gate)?

I am here to help you explore what the narrow gate experience may be like. If you decide that it's not for you, no harm no foul. You can return to the mundane routine of church religion rather than embracing the true excitement of following Christ. The choice is yours, but at least you'll be making the choice this time rather than doing what's always been done because you were taught it was right.

Use the space below to reflect on and answer these questions for yourself. You can answer them now or come back to them later.

In what ways do you fall in the Christianese camp?

_____

_____

_____

What religious traditions do you hold dear?

_____

_____

_____

What evidence of God do you see in your life?

_____

_____

_____

In what areas of your faith are you the strongest?

_____

_____

_____

_____

In what areas of your faith are you the weakest?

_____

_____

_____

_____

Use this space for taking additional notes or
journaling your thoughts.

_____

_____

_____

_____

_____

_____

_____

_____

_____

_____

_____

_____

_____

"Two roads diverged in a wood, and I—
I took the one less traveled by,
And that has made all the difference."

Excerpt taken from Robert Frost's poem
entitled "The Road not Taken"

5

MY JOURNEY THROUGH THE NARROW GATE

My first indication that I was just a churchgoer and not a true Christian Believer was the lack of scripture I knew. I had no confidence in going out to witness because I lacked true knowledge. I couldn't share the gospel for real. I had no relationship with God. In fact, the only prayer I said was a blessing over my food and I usually forgot to do that! I only knew about the church! Of course, I could summarize a few Bible stories that I had heard growing up, but I had not taken the time to read anything for myself, and I knew something had to change.

My next clue that I was a churchgoer was the fact that I could list all of my accomplishments related to serving in the church: youth usher, youth choir, youth group, etc., but I knew nothing about the church and the Christian faith and how it was developed. I had no accomplishments regarding my walk for Christ. I knew no history outside of what I was taught in public school.

I could not tell you how the different denominations developed, I knew little about how Christianity spread, or how influential the gospel message was to our political, economic, and geographic climates. For all I knew, Christianity was the white man's religion that was introduced to us in slavery, and Jesus really did look like a European, same as the present-day Jews in Israel. I thought I could just do good and keep going to church. In other words, my faith had no backing and no foundational support- it was built on sand!

After all this reflection, I was disappointed in myself for perpetrating. I sounded Christian and acted Christian, but I was a fake. I had allowed myself to make church my priority.

My validations in so many areas of life centered around church and the people there. Church was my God because it mattered more to me than Christ. I was a grown adult physically but still a babe in Christ spiritually.

I used the very resources at my fingertips as a starting point- the church. This time, my heart was postured with Jesus Christ in the center, and
I was focused on uncovering the truth for myself. At that time, I was in my last semester of college, and I had just joined a new church. I took a slew of their biblical studies classes on different topics like spiritual warfare, prioritizing God, and understanding God. I had a hunger to know God and He honored that in so many ways. He catapulted my growth over those next few years.

I became empowered to make a change, to know the God of the Bible for myself, and to become a better Christian.

The following year, I enrolled in a 24- week discipleship class called Masterlife and began to teach it for several sessions after that. The more I studied, the more the Word got in me and came out of me.

My confidence grew and I was transformed from the inside. Who I was at church became who I was at home and then at work and school. My identity as a Christian was on a firm foundation.

One year in particular, I decided to combine my love for history and the Word and embarked on a journey to read the Bible in a year, the chronological NLT version. This was the next level for me! All the stories I had known and heard made complete sense because I was able to read the Bible in order of events. At the same time, I was also in graduate school and taking courses like hermeneutics (how to study the Bible) and church history. Now, all the information I knew fit together like glue, and I started to question church religion more and more.

Like why didn't I learn the history of the church in church? Why wasn't I aware that the holidays we value in the 21st century come from the Catholic faith's recognition of saints? If the Bible shows us how many years the earth has existed and that evolution is distorted, why do we let our children believe that it has existed for millions of years just because "science" says so? What is the reason we celebrate religious holidays that have nothing to do with Jesus Christ- are Easter eggs, trunk or treats, and Santa Claus necessary?

The more I learned from reading the Bible, being led by God, watching documentaries, listening to sound doctrine, etc. the more I realized that this church religion was not serving me well. At first, I was comfortable with not participating and volunteering in certain activities the church hosted, but then I realized it still had an influence on me, and I knew at some point soon God would call me away completely.

Yes, I loved the people and cared for them dearly, but I knew in my heart that this institution was built on rocky and thorny soil- it has no deep roots and is crowded out by life (see Matthew 13 for full reference). Jesus was included but the focus was not on Him. If it were, then EVERYTHING would be centered on biblical principles and the fruit would be evident in the lives of all members. The church religion has temporary fruit. There is no lasting deliverance, no evidence of miracles, and most importantly no sensitivity to the Spirit.

It is important to note here that although I was on an evolving journey, God was with me the entire time- from my "babe in Christ days" to my "making disciples days". God is with us even when we are not fully at our best, but He's not okay with us staying there.

Once the COVID-19 pandemic hit and I witnessed first-hand the lack of faith among churchgoers across the nation who let their lives be led by fear, I knew it was time to part ways. They weren't reading and embracing the Word of God and living by His command. The church religion was not fruitful and was no longer feeding me well.

With God's guidance, I had already been developing a community of my own on the back end that would prepare me for this phase; so, it's not like I left the church and went to nothing. I had already been teaching Bible Study online for quite some time, participating in Bible book groups, weekly biblical meditations, solo worship nights, and journaling and studying with the Holy Spirit. Not to mention, I slowly started following other preachers and prophets who aligned better with my focus and taught the deep content that I needed more understanding about.

All of this happened because I decided to learn more, read for myself, and trust God. I let go of people-pleasing and every other toxic mindset that I needed to break to better understand God and serve Him letter. I let God guide me; I let Him expose and teach me. No matter how many times I discovered that the truth has really been intentionally hidden, I kept going because I did not want the "ignorance is bliss" mentality. I knew that the truth was the only thing that would set me free, and I have sought and continue to seek it every day.

Ask and it will be given to you; seek and you will find; knock and the door will be opened to you. For everyone who asks receives; the one who seeks finds; and to the one who knocks, the door will be opened. Matthew 7:7-8, NIV

Now your journey may be different from mine, but the destination is the same- a true authentic experience with God. We can no longer live on the faith of our ancestors, nor can we blame our past for our present because God is giving us all the opportunity to invite Him in to our hearts and lives.

Use this space to journal about the traditions you are struggling with letting go of and the emotions you feel right now.

_____

_____

_____

_____

_____

_____

_____

_____

_____

_____

_____

_____

_____

_____

_____

_____

_____

_____

_____

6

THE CHOICE IS YOURS

Some people are afraid of the truth so they will choose to avoid having their own journey with God. I am urging you not to be this type of person. Your salvation is on the line, and Paul advises us to work out our own salvation.

Therefore, my dear friends, as you have always obeyed- not only in my presence, but now much more in my absence- continue to work out your salvation with fear and trembling, for it is God who works in you to will and to act in order to fulfill his good purpose. Philippians 2:12-13

I may be happy with my progress, but I can't stand to sit by and watch others stay stuck in the cycles of insanity when they can have a true genuine relationship with Jesus Christ. Our families don't have to be broken, our finances don't have to operate in lack, our health doesn't have to be in danger, and our minds don't have to be in bondage. We need to get our spiritual lives in order so we can properly address the issues in our lives and live abundantly.

Being a Christian means that you are a follower of Jesus Christ, Messiah, the Anointed One. Your life in every way should reflect that you submit to Christ. Simply being a member of a church won't get you there, staying busy in serving at the church won't get you there, knowing how to do church well will never equate to being a Christian Believer. It starts with a true decision to learn for yourself and let the Holy Spirit guide you from there (this includes all the unlearning of culture and toxic doctrine you'll go through).

I am not encouraging others to leave their church, I'm just encouraging you to grow up in Christ. Go learn God for yourself; there are a plethora of quality resources available to you regardless of your starting point (I have included a small list at the end of this book).

The apostle Paul refers to it as craving pure spiritual milk. Trust that God will lead your way through the Narrow Gate.

Are you really content with knowing that there is more to your faith that you have yet to tap into simply because you choose not to learn it? Do you trust your church more than you trust God? We, the true church, as in the body of Christ, are His bride. The church religion that we are currently participating in is far beyond Christ's idea of a bride submitted to Him. We do not look nor act like Christians. Don't take my word for it, evaluate it for yourself with scripture. This is what the true church is supposed to be like, a body of people dedicated to our union with Christ.

Therefore, rid yourselves of all malice and all deceit, hypocrisy, envy, and slander of every kind. Like newborn babies, crave pure spiritual milk, so that by it you may grow up in your salvation, now that you have tasted that the Lord is good. 1 Peter 2:1-3, NIV

Submit to one another out of reverence for Christ. Wives, submit yourselves to your own husbands as you do to the Lord. For the husband is the head of the wife as Christ is the head of the church, his body, of which he is the Savior. Now as the church submits to Christ, so also wives should submit to their husbands in everything.

Husbands, love your wives, just as Christ loved the church and gave himself up for her to make her holy, cleansing her by the washing with water through the word, and to present her to himself as a radiant church, without stain or wrinkle or any other blemish, but holy and blameless. In this same way, husbands ought to love their wives as their own bodies.

He who loves his wife loves himself. After all, no one ever hated their own body, but they feed and care for their body, just as Christ does the church- for we are members of his body. For this reason a man will leave his father and mother and be united to his wife, and the two will become one flesh. This is a profound mystery- but I am talking about Christ and the church. However, each one of you also must love his wife as he loves himself, and the wife must respect her husband.

Ephesians 5: 21-33

SO, WHAT NOW?

If this seems like a daunting process, let me reassure you with some boundaries that were helpful for me.

1) You must have your own regular time with God and His Word. Focus on building this as a habit. Not just to say you've completed it, but to commune regularly with God.

This is the crux of being able to mature within your individual relationship.

This time should be free from distractions, and the only routine is to have it. It may look like more worship and prayer than reading and journaling on some days and that is good.

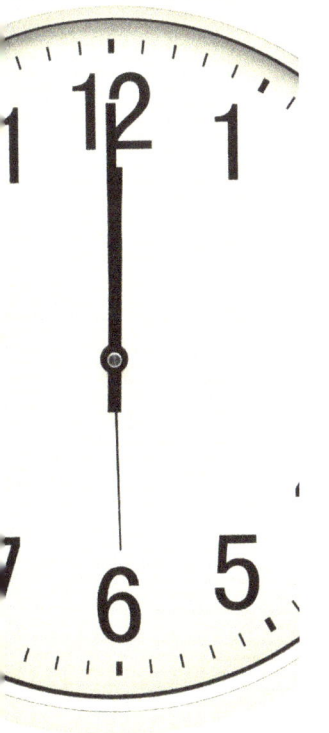

Strict routines don't leave room for flexibility. There are two consistent questions that I learned to answer from my days in Masterlife that I will recommend for you when spending time in the Word.

- What is God saying to you? This open-ended question leaves room for you to reflect about the message God is communicating to you through the text.
- What are you saying to God? This question causes you to focus on your response to God so that you can align with His will.

2) Recognize when you're entering an information overload zone. This is when you have little focus on what's at hand because you can barely process the information as it's coming at you. You need to slow down, regroup, and turn off the media. It's easy to get down a rabbit hole when you're curious about a research topic, but consistency not speed is the key.

Sometimes we can overload on You Tube sermons, Google articles, and podcasts. Try driving or working in silence for a while, this usually helps your brain reset so you can be prepared to receive the information and file it away properly. You won't have all the answers upfront, but trust that God will show you when it's time.

3) Take regular days of rest, preferably the Sabbath (Saturdays). In modern culture, we are taught to do it all and stay busy, yet the one thing we do poorly is rest. Sleep in, spend time in prayer, go for a walk, make no plans for the day, watch useful content, eat good food, but DO NOT WORK! This has so many benefits, including communing with God in the smallest ways. You'll find yourself being more grateful for life and His creation and under-standing the importance of simplicity. Once you get used to resting (yes, there is an adjustment period), you'll wish you had always done this!

What happens if I mess up along the way?

Repent to God, let it go, and try again. Get back into your days of rest, developing boundaries, and your regular time with God. Do not make this complicated. Do not overthink things. Day by day you will find that life is easier because you are trusting God to guide you and you are learning and growing.

If you enter this season with the expectation of growing beyond your imagination, your faith will not waver. Expect the unexpected, be open to grieving your past while enjoying the present journey, build new communities along the way, pray about everything, learn from others but always test it by the Spirit, focus on consistency with your disciplines, and remember that the point of all of this is to grow your faith and relationship with God.

I can truly say that I am much happier on this side of it all. I would not trade my relationship with God for anything or anyone. He has strengthened what was weak, pruned what was not growing, cut off what was not good, multiplied my efforts, and transformed my life. He can do the same for you.

Now that you have a better grasp of your options, it's time to decide-

Narrow Gate or Wide Gate?

"Enter through the narrow gate. For wide is the gate and broad is the road that leads to destruction, and many enter through it. But small is the gate and narrow the road that leads to life, and only a few find it." Matthew 7: 13-14, NIV

*Use this space for taking additional notes or
journaling your thoughts.*

_____

_____

_____

_____

_____

_____

_____

_____

_____

_____

_____

_____

_____

_____

_____

_____

_____

_____

_____

_____

_____

Thank you for taking the time to read this book. The following page provides some resources to get you started in growing your relationship with Jesus Christ. Please be sure to seek the Lord regarding every step of your journey. Trust that He holds you even as you wrestle in the spirit with new understanding. Read your Bible and pray everyday.

As quoted in Numbers 6:24-26, "'The Lord bless you and keep you; the Lord make his face shine on you and be gracious to you; the Lord turn his face toward you and give you peace. Amen.

> God never said that the journey would be easy, but He did say that the arrival would be worthwhile.
>
> -Max Lucado

RESOURCES

Apps & Sites to Follow

The Bible App
(listen to audio of Bible
being read aloud)

The Bible Project
You Tube Channel

Books to Read

Placebo by Howard Pittman
(pdf available online)

Getting on Higher Ground
Devotional and Journal
highergroundconsulting.co/shop

Influential You Tube
Movies to Watch

The Last Reformation: The Life
Prophet Suddenly

Jessica T. Grier

Author, Speaker, Coach

🌐 highergroundconsulting.co

Follow me @gettingonhigherground

MEET JESSICA

Jessica T. Grier is an author, counselor, Bible teacher, and servant. She designed the concept of Kingdom Wellness Coaching as a unique approach to help Christian Believers align their whole selves to God's intention for their wellbeing. She coaches believers in developing a Kingdom based mindset so that every area of life is aligned to God's Word.

Jessica is currently licensed as an Associate Professional Counselor and works as a certified Middle School Counselor. She is a graduate of Richmont Graduate University (M.A.) and Spelman College (B.A.). She has taught a bi-weekly virtual Bible study for women and a biblical studies course, known as Masterlife, in her local church. She continues to seek new ways to share the Word of God as an author, speaker, and coach. She is married and lives in the Metro Atlanta area with her husband.

Scan the QR code or go to highergroundconsulting.co to learn more about Jessica

Did you book your call?

Kingdom Wellness

Planning Session

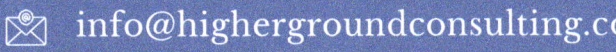 info@highergroundconsulting.co

🌐 www.highergroundconsulting.co

Visit calendly.com/gettingonhigherground

Jessica T. Grier

**Kingdom
Wellness Coach**

Jessica T. Grier
Author, Speaker, Coach
🌐 highergroundconsulting.co
Follow me @gettingonhigherground

ADDITIONAL AUTHOR WORKS

Book Bio

Getting On Higher Ground is a 365- day devotional developed to expose Believers to the diversity of God's Word and to help them understand it in practical ways. Each day provides a 3-minute scripture reading and reflection piece to aid in daily growth.

SHOUTOUT ATLANTA   VoyageATL

Book Highlights:
This devotional helps Christian Believers:

- Spark a desire to read the Bible daily
- Improve their understanding of scripture and memorization
- Develop an intimate relationship with God by providing daily scripture, reflection, and journaling.
- Focus on self-care with monthly coloring pages included

Jessica T. Grier
Author, Speaker, Coach

🌐 highergroundconsulting.co

Follow me @gettingonhigherground

AUTHOR WORKS CONT.

Book Bio

Along with taking a moment for biblical meditation using the *Getting On Higher Ground* 365-day devotional, it is helpful to embrace the practice of journaling your thoughts and reactions to God's Word. Use this journal to write about God's Word, your prayers, and thoughts about how to apply His Word to your everyday life. Commune with God on a higher level than ever before.

An intentional free-write space for embracing God's Word in your daily life!

Scan the QR Code or visit highergroundconsulting.co/shop to place your order!

Jessica T. Grier

Author, Speaker, Coach

🌐 highergroundconsulting.co
E-mail: info@highergroundconsulting.co

BOOK ME TO SPEAK!

Empowering Christian women to apply practical wisdom for optimal wellbeing.

"I remember a time in my life when I knew I believed in God but did not see the evidence of much faith in my lifestyle. My relationships were surface-level, my finances were lacking, and I was emotionally frustrated and angry underneath my mask. This led to having no lasting impact for the Kingdom of God. I want to help Believers bridge the gap between what they believe and how they live so that every Believer has a true relationship with God and flourishes as a Kingdom citizen."

Speaker Topics:

- How To Uncomplicate Your Life and Simplify Priorities
- Culture Correcting: How to Overcome Your Identity Crisis
- I'm not "Superwoman", Embracing Your True Self

Speaking engagements catered to girls and women 11 and older